1

29,

2

4

17

GREAT CENTRAL RAILWAY

MATT ALLEN

HALSGROVE

First published in Great Britain in 2009

British Library Cataloguing-in-Publication Data
A CIP record for this title is available from the British Library

ISBN 978 1 84114 898 4

HALSGROVE
Halsgrove House,
Ryelands Industrial Estate,
Bagley Road, Wellington, Somerset TA21 9PZ
Tel: 01823 653777   Fax: 01823 216796
email: sales@halsgrove.com

Part of the Halsgrove group of companies
Information on all Halsgrove titles is available at: www.halsgrove.com

Printed and bound by Grafiche Flaminia, Italy

FOREWORD

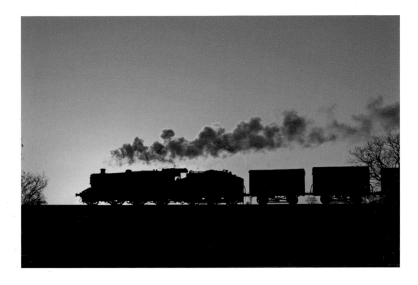

Looking at our heritage railway today, it is tempting to take the scene for granted. Double track, large locomotives, diverse freight trains being checked at grand looking signals. It is everything that our preservation founders decreed it should be. A section of main line railway where classic steam designs could be showcased. That original meeting took place forty years ago in a waiting room at Leicester Central Station when the final closure of the Great Central was announced.

This book is perfectly timed. What better occasion than our fortieth anniversary to bring together a selection of evocative images? They serve to remind us, while we've got our section of main line and some magnificent locomotives (now including some immaculate heritage diesels!) we can never take it for granted. What has been achieved has been built by the hard work and determination of many people across four decades. They have all shared the vision and contributed to the GCR's growth and survival.

There's still much to do. We'd very much like to extend northwards from Loughborough. Our sister operation already operates trains on another section of the line heading towards Nottingham. If we could join them not only would our main line be longer but it could be a world-renowned attraction, an asset for the East Midlands.

What is certain is we will only continue to achieve our ambitions with your support. We owe our thanks to all of our visitors in the last forty years. To everyone who has joined our membership club, bought shares or donated to our charity (The David Clarke Railway Trust), thank you for making a personal commitment to the Great Central adventure. It has given me great pleasure to write this and spend some moments reflecting. I wonder who will introduce our 80th anniversary book? More importantly – what wonderful achievements will they look back on?

Bill Ford
GCR President
April 2009.

INTRODUCTION

In this book, the Halsgrove Railway series takes us to Leicestershire to see a real heritage main line, the Great Central Railway. It is unique as the only double track heritage railway in the UK, so you can be travelling through the Leicestershire countryside steam-style and pass another steam hauled train traveling in the opposite direction, just like yesteryear. The Great Central Railway (GCR) is one of Leicestershire's most popular tourist attractions, hosting around 100,000 visitors each year.

This book will take you on a photographic journey along the eight-mile line starting at the university town of Loughborough and running through to Leicester North. You'll see great collection of locomotives, historic rolling stock and the restored period stations. Some of the photographs also catch that 'lucky moment' when two steam trains pass each other at speed.

The railway which became known as the Great Central began its life 1864 as the Manchester, Sheffield and Lincolnshire Railway (MS&LR). Edward Watkin, the general manager and latterly the chairman of the railway, had a grand vision: linking the rail centres of Sheffield and Manchester with mainland Europe through a 'Channel Tunnel' no less! This vision never came to fruition, but a main line route from Manchester, Sheffield and Nottingham to London was constructed. The railway changed its name to the Great Central in 1897 and the line to London (known as the London extension) opened in 1899 at a cost of £11.5 million. In 1923 the railway became a part of the London and North Eastern Railway (LNER) and when nationalisation beckoned in 1948 it became a part of British Railways Eastern Region.

As with many railways the rapid march of the motor vehicle began to hit the economics of the railway hard. By the 1950s the line was under threat – unfortunately the Great Central was an easy target as other railway lines also served the big towns and cities on its route. A gradual rundown of services culminated with large stretches of line being closed in 1966, the final Nottingham to Rugby section closing in 1969.

Despite the closure by British Railways, a group of railway enthusiasts were keen not to see the Great Central disappear into history. The line was re-opened in 1974, initially running to Quorn and Woodhouse and shortly after to Rothley. The most southerly point, Leicester North, was reached in 1989 and the station there opened in 1991. Initially the railway re-opened as a single track line but the project to make the line double track (as far as Rothley) was finally completed in 2000. The railway continues to move forward with some big projects planned. The 'Top Shed' project involves moving a complete engine shed from Workington in Cumbria to Loughborough. The engine shed has already been dismantled and will be another major attraction in its own right once re-erected at the Great Central. The 'Bridging the Gap' project is another long term goal, which involves re-instating a bridge over the Midland Mainline to connect up with the Great Central Railway Northern Heritage Railway at Ruddington. Further expansion of the line is also planned with the Swithland to Mountsorrel branch line.

The 'new' Great Central Railway is a fantastic step back in time; for me the atmosphere created by the double track operation and mainline stations makes the GCR a different experience to any other heritage railway.

The railway has a great selection of locomotives and rolling stock, much of which you will see in this book. Some of the non-passenger vehicles are of great interest, for example the fully restored Travelling Post Office train which you may see in operation at special events through the year. The railway also has a wide selection of freight wagons which are used for demonstration purposes on a regular basis. Although the railway has no rail connection to the main network rail system, visiting locomotives can be brought in by road to complement the home fleet.

Whilst trains are restricted to 25mph, in common with other heritage railways, the GCR is also unique in having permission to run certain trains (mainly for testing purposes) at 60mph. This means occasional contract work is undertaken to test a variety of modern and heritage locomotives.

This book would not be possible without all the volunteers who put in thousands of hours to make the Great Central what it is today. It is a striking thought that it takes tens of thousands of hours to perform a heavy overhaul on a steam locomotive. I thank them for ensuring the rest of us can enjoy the railway as we see it today.

If you haven't paid a visit to the railway, hopefully this book will convince you that a visit is a must. Maybe try one of their fantastic dining trains, or a special gala day to see the Travelling Post Office in action, or simply enjoy a leisurely ride along the line remembering to look out for that special moment when a steam train passes in the opposite direction.

This is 'Halsgrove Railway Series Double Track Style'. Take your seat and let the journey commence. . .

Matt Allen
Basingstoke
Feb 2009

GREAT CENTRAL RAILWAY
LOUGHBOROUGH, LEICESTERSHIRE

THE GREAT CENTRAL RAILWAY

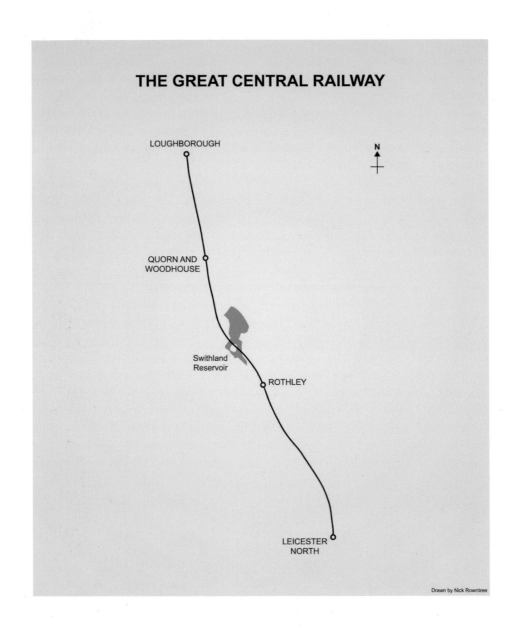

LOUGHBOROUGH

QUORN AND
WOODHOUSE

Swithland
Reservoir

ROTHLEY

LEICESTER
NORTH

N

Drawn by Nick Rowntree

Loughborough Station is the beginning of the line. Here Q6 locomotive number 63395 is waiting to depart with a demonstration freight train. This locomotive was visiting the railway from its home on the North Yorkshire Moors Railway. *Photograph by Matt Allen.*

Quite literally the difference between night and day! Taken in the same spot as the previous photograph, another locomotive that visited the railway was Stanier Mogul number 42968. *Photograph by Warwick Falconer.*

The view from the northern end of the platform at Loughborough. To the right you can see various diesel locomotives whilst the steam shed is beyond the bridge in the distance. *Photograph by Matt Allen.*

Loughborough Station is of classic Great Central Railway design, a central island platform with tracks either side, access from the road being via a central staircase (visible in this picture). *Photograph by Matt Allen.*

The station has lots of period artefacts and features giving it a real 'Steam Era' feel. In fact Loughborough Station has been restored to the BR era of the 1950s. *Photograph by Matt Allen.*

Another 'after dark' shot. The train in the platform is one of the railway's regular dining trains – in a couple of hours' time the station will be bustling with activity as people board. Steam by night is a truly magical affair, good food and wine making the experience even more enjoyable! *Photograph by Matt Allen.*

During an organised photographers' event a member of the footplate crew has been persuaded to help create a timeless scene. *Photograph by Matt Allen.*

Hidden at the south end of Loughborough Station is a
great museum full of historic items. *Photograph by Matt Allen.*

In the window of the museum is this tribute to David Clarke, a long time supporter and financial backer of the Great Central Railway. His contribution to the railway has played a large part it making what you see today possible. The 'David Clarke Railway Trust' is a charity set up in his name to support the railway. *Photograph by Matt Allen*.

The Late David Clarke
President & Benefactor
Great Central Railway

The engine shed at Loughborough is a busy place; both long-term restoration projects and routine maintenance are carried out here. Resident BR Standard class 2, number 78019 can be seen waiting its next duty.
Photograph by Matt Allen.

16

30777 'Sir Lamiel' is a King Arthur class locomotive and would have spent its British Railways days at home on the Southern Region. It's seen here being prepared for a steam gala weekend where the railway runs a very intensive service.
Photograph by Matt Allen.

Left:
The train crew consisting of fireman, driver and guard discuss the day ahead, prior to leaving Loughborough. *Photograph by Matt Allen.*

Right:
O4 class locomotive 63601 is 'running around' its train at Loughborough. The railway doesn't currently have a turntable, so it's simply a case of taking the engine off one end and moving in to the other. Note the water tower in the background.
Photograph by Matt Allen.

Below:
The Great Central Railway has a great relationship with the National Railway Museum and is the custodian of a number of their locomotives. The locomotive in question here is 30777 'Sir Lamiel'. *Photograph by Matt Allen.*

Above:
Another scene from a photographers' event, featuring Super D number 49395 and 8F 48305. This view is looking south. *Photograph by Matt Allen.*

Right:
Taken from just under the bridge in the previous photograph a daytime view looking south from the station. The double track (meaning there are two adjacent tracks so trains can pass each other on the move) leads to a quite complex arrangement of track and signalling. *Photograph by Matt Allen.*

Left:
'Approaching Loughborough', taken from the footplate of 8F locomotive 48305, a resident of the railway.
Photograph by Matt Allen.

Far left:
'Loughborough Departure', Britannia number 70048 (actually 70013 in disguise) begins the journey to Leicester North. The main station building can be seen at road level emblazoned with 'Great Central Railway'.
Photograph by Matt Allen.

The railway has probably the biggest selection of heritage freight wagons in the UK which can often be seen in use at special events. Here another long term resident 63601 heads a train of mixed freight wagons. *Photograph by Matt Allen.*

Another National Railway Museum-owned locomotive that visited the railway for a short period was 850 'Lord Nelson'. Resplendent in 'Malachite Green' it's seen here waiting to depart the siding just south of Loughborough Station. *Photograph by Matt Allen*.

Black 5 number 45305 is normally seen at home on the GCR; in this picture the locomotive has been renumbered 45292 recreating the last train to run on the original GCR before closure by British Railways. The word 'Last' can just be seen chalked onto the smokebox door. *Photograph by Matt Allen.*

BR Standard Tank number 80105 is normally resident at the Bo'Ness and Kinneil railway in Scotland so is a long way from home in this photograph. *Photograph by Matt Allen.*

Merchant Navy Class locomotive 35030 'Elder Dempster Lines' (actually 35005 'Canadian Pacific')
waits its next duty outside Loughborough Station. *Photograph by Matt Allen.*

Whilst utilising predominantly steam power the railway has a good selection of diesels to complement the steam fleet. Here the Class 101 DMU is seen passing under the signals at Beeches Road nearing the end of its journey to Loughborough. *Photograph by Matt Allen.*

The signals at Beeches Road provide photographers with a real treat, creating lots of added interest. 78019 is making a rather spirited departure on a cold winter's day. *Photograph by Matt Allen.*

Taken from the other side of the line 30777 'Sir Lamiel' is seen with the 'Travelling Post Office Train'. *Photograph by Matt Allen*.

A pair of English Electric Class 20 locomotives complete with 'Jolly Fisherman' headboard featured during a 'Seaside Specials Gala Event'. The locomotives have an interesting design with a single cab at one end, and are often seen together in pairs like this. *Photograph by Matt Allen.*

73129 is a British Railways Standard 5 Class locomotive but is very unusual in being fitted with Caprotti valve gear. The engine was making a rare visit from its home base at the Midland Railway Centre to the Great Central. *Photograph by Warwick Falconer.*

Left:
'Tornado', 60163 is the first steam locomotive to be built in the UK for over 40 years. No A1 Class locomotives were preserved so the A1 Steam Trust set about building their own locomotive from scratch to the original design, an incredible feat. The locomotive was used for the very first time at the GCR where it spent a few months being 'run in'. Interestingly the locomotive remained in grey undercoat for its running-in period.
Photograph by Matt Allen.

Right:
GWR Hall Class locomotive number 4953 'Pitchford Hall' is normally resident at Tyseley Locomotive Works, and is seen here on a visit to the line. This locomotive was built at Swindon Works in 1929 at a cost of £4375.
Photograph by Matt Allen.

Above:
63601 creates a lovely exhaust as it accelerates under the
signals at Beeches Road. *Photograph by Matt Allen.*

Left:
70013 'Oliver Cromwell' has recently been returned to steam with the
heavy overhaul being carried out at the Great Central, on behalf of the
National Railway Museum who own this wonderful engine. The engine
has been overhauled to 'Mainline Standard' so can often be seen
hauling steam specials all over the UK. *Photograph by Matt Allen.*

Taken further down the line on a summer's day. Fairburn Tank number 42085 is normally based at the Lakeside and Haverthwaite Railway and is seen here making a very rare visit from its home in the Lake District. It was actually at Loughborough to have some heavy repairs carried out but the opportunity was taken to use it on a steam gala weekend. *Photograph by Matt Allen.*

The same location as the previous photograph but looking in the opposite direction.
The 8F numbered 48188 is actually home-based 48305 in disguise. As you would expect for a mainline, the railway has very few curves or bends the majority of the line being extremely straight.
This can be seen clearly on this photograph. *Photograph by Matt Allen.*

Again the same location as the previous two photographs, with the footbridge that crosses the line giving a different perspective. You can see Beeches Road Bridge in the background as 78019 passes a freight train. *Photograph by Matt Allen.*

The railway boasts a good selection of diesel locomotives. Here D123 'Sherwood Forrester' is producing an exhaust like a steam locomotive! *Photograph by Matt Allen.*

30777 'Sir Lamiel' with matching Southern Region green coaches makes a great sight. 30777 is another locomotive which has recently undergone a heavy overhaul at the Great Central at great financial cost. *Photograph by Matt Allen*.

78019 passes under the footbridge, which provided a great vantage point for the earlier photograph. The lovely winter light brings the scene to life. *Photograph by Matt Allen.*

Above:
Autumn. With the autumn colours beginning to show 'Lord Nelson' number 850 is approaching the A6 road bridge. *Photograph by Matt Allen.*

Right:
Summer. An amazing contrast to the previous photograph, the summer colours creating this very bright scene with 7821 'Ditcheat Manor' producing great smoke effects. *Photograph by Warwick Falconer.*

Winter. Completing the trio of photographs showing how the seasons dramatically change the look of the railway, Q6 number 63396 passes a passenger train heading towards Loughborough. The rear coach just visible is an ex-LMS Inspection Saloon. *Photograph by Matt Allen*.

Heavy freight locomotive 9F number 92212 is seen heading north towards Loughborough. The locomotive was based at the Great Central for a number of years but can now be seen on the Mid Hants Railway. *Photograph by Warwick Falconer.*

Jubilee Class locomotive number 5690 'Leander' was a colourful visitor to the railway. This engine is a regular on 'the Big Railway' being passed to work specials on the mainline across the UK. *Photograph by Matt Allen.*

The final photograph in this selection around the A6 road bridge catches 48305 in powerful mood. *Photograph by Warwick Falconer.*

Above:
A case of being in the right place at the right time! You have to be very lucky to catch the moment two trains pass each other; here D123 is heading towards Loughborough with 63601 heading south. *Photograph by Matt Allen.*

Left:
Woodthorpe is one of the most popular locations along the line for photographers. 'Oliver Cromwell' heads a mixed train of green and red/cream coaches. *Photograph by Matt Allen.*

51

30777 is caught on a steam gala day when the railway runs a very intensive service. The spire which adds some added interest at this location is actually Loughborough Crematorium.
Photograph by Matt Allen.

The same location as the previous photograph but seen from the other side of the line. 78019 is hauling a dining train on a lovely summer evening.
Photograph by Matt Allen.

Black 5 45305 has been a regular on the Great Central for a number of years. The locomotive paired with its maroon coaches creates a perfect British Railways era train, next stop Marylebone. . .
Photograph by Matt Allen.

63601 on a beautiful autumn day.
Photograph by Warwick Falconer.

The bridge at Woodthorpe not only provides a good vantage point but also some added interest when included in the photograph. *Photograph by Warwick Falconer.*

With stormy skies gathering, 63395, a genuine heavy freight engine, looks very much the part with its train of 'windcutter' wagons. This photograph was taken on a photographers' charter. *Photograph by Matt Allen.*

The original 'Irish Mail' ran between London Euston and Holyhead; this train could have feasibly diverted via the Great Central. 45305 is at the head of the train in this recreation. *Photograph by Warwick Falconer.*

Same location, different day. On a very wet and grey day a photographers' charter was held that featured two freight trains. Super 43995 on the mixed freight and 8F 48305 on the windcutters facing in opposite directions. Trying to choreograph two trains passing at exactly the right point is harder than it looks. *Photograph by Matt Allen.*

Caught at speed. 48773 (actually 48305) is approaching Woodthorpe.
The yellow stripe across the cab was a designation during the late
steam days of British Railways that the locomotive should
not go south of Crewe. *Photograph by Matt Allen.*

Lovely light on a winter afternoon sees Scottish visitor 80105 working towards its first stop at Quorn and Woodhouse. *Photograph by Warwick Falconer.*

With a headcode of 2A22 Class 31 diesel number D5830 passes Woodthorpe on a lovely summer's day. This locomotive was built at the nearby Loughborough Brush Works in 1962 and now carries this striking 'Golden Ochre' livery. *Photograph by Matt Allen*.

42968 passes under the road bridge with a train of box vans. 42968 is a firm favourite with rail enthusiasts and makes quite a few visits to various railways (as seen here) from its home based at the Severn Valley Railway. *Photograph by Warwick Falconer.*

92212 is seen heading north towards Loughborough with the windcutter rake of mineral wagons. This locomotive had a shockingly short life under British Railways, being built in September 1959 and withdrawn a mere eight years later. *Photograph by Matt Allen.*

Judging by the 'restaurant car' at the front of the train, 42968 is hauling a lunchtime dining train south. *Photograph by Warwick Falconer.*

'Oliver Cromwell' at the head of a rather short van train. The 'Brit' (short for Britannia) was one of the last steam locomotives to run on British Railways lasting until the end of steam in 1968. *Photograph by Matt Allen.*

A pair of fives. Black 5 number 45305 is being piloted by Standard 5 number 73129. It is interesting to note the different British Railways emblems on the tenders, the lead engine having the earlier version. *Photograph by Matt Allen.*

On a summer's day 78019 is approaching the Loughborough bypass road bridge. This 2MT locomotive is perfect for a heritage railway, a great compromise between power and cost effective running. *Photograph by Warwick Falconer.*

An amazing contrast to the previous photograph, the same location but on a snowy winter's day, 63601 heads a short passenger train. *Photograph by Warwick Falconer.*

44422 is a 4F 0-6-0 freight locomotive, although they would have been seen on passenger trains in British Railways service. The engine was built at Derby Locomotive Works in 1927 and its first allocation was at Leicester shed, so is back at home on the GCR. *Photograph by Warwick Falconer.*

A winter frost and bright blue skies, pure heaven for a railway photographer. Small Prairie number 5199 seems to be making good progress passing Woodthorpe. The spire of the crematorium is just visible to the left of the locomotive. *Photograph by Warwick Falconer.*

During special gala events the diesel locomotives also get a chance to haul demonstration freight trains. *Photograph by Matt Allen.*

A final photograph at Woodthorpe seeing 60163 in fine form. Striking in its grey undercoat the brand new A1 was a huge attraction; its visit to the GCR was a huge coup for the railway. *Photograph by Matt Allen.*

The next stop on our journey is the approach to Quorn and Woodhouse Station; here the line opens out with farmland either side of the line. Passenger trains are likely to be slowing at this point, where demonstration freight trains (as seen here) will still be working hard as they won't be stopping at the station. 42968 seems to be in fine form. *Photograph by Warwick Falconer.*

Above:
The early morning light in this location can be lovely, something photographers can exploit during special events when the train service starts earlier than usual. 78019 is heading towards Quorn and Woodhouse with short mixed freight. *Photograph by Matt Allen.*

Left:
The approach to Quorn and Woodhouse is one of the places on the line where a silhouette shot is possible, 63995 making a fine sight. *Photograph by Matt Allen.*

A rather unusual view taken from the brake van on a minerals train. The locomotive heading the train is 8F 48305. *Photograph by Matt Allen.*

The fields on the east side of the line present lots of options for the photographer, where many different positions are enhanced with a stream and in this case some sheep. The train engine is 30777. *Photograph by Warwick Falconer.*

70013 picks up the early morning light as it heads south. *Photograph by Matt Allen.*

This day was so grey and wet that the colour photograph looked pretty much black and white! A truly timeless scene, somehow the grey conditions adding to the atmosphere as Super D number 49395 is seen heading south. *Photograph by Matt Allen.*

The GCR is a fairly flat railway, the milepost indicates gradients of 1 in 330 and 1in 176. Most locomotives at the railway face south, however in this case 48773 (actually 48305) is facing north seen here accelerating towards Loughborough. *Photograph by Matt Allen.*

63601 was built in 1911 and is an original Great Central Railway locomotive, returning to its roots since preservation. *Photograph by Matt Allen.*

Above:
As trains enter the Quorn and Woodhouse Station complex there
are some more fine signals. 63601 is just approaching the station.
Photograph by Matt Allen.

Left:
A very colourful silhouette with 4953 accelerating towards
Quorn and Woodhouse with a Travelling Post Office Train
on a late winter's afternoon. *Photograph by Matt Allen.*

35030 (actually 35005) is heading north from Quorn Station. 35030 ran a railtour over the Great Central on 3rd September 1966 a few days before original closure of the line. The photographers' special seen is this photograph is a recreation of that train. *Photograph by Warwick Falconer.*

4141 is a resident of the line, seen here taking part in a 'Windcutters Gala' where the windcutters mineral wagons saw extensive use. *Photograph by Matt Allen.*

Above:
42968 is picking up some lovely winter light as it heads towards Quorn
with a train of box vans. *Photograph by Warwick Falconer.*

Right:
For the centenary of the Territorial Army in 2008 'Oliver Cromwell' was disguised as its
long gone classmate 70048, which was called 'Territorial Army'. *Photograph by Matt Allen.*

In lovely winter light the two Type 2 class 20s approach Quorn and Woodhouse Station. This class of locomotive was withdrawn from British Railways in the late '80s and early '90s having seen over 40 years of service. *Photograph by Matt Allen*.

70013 accelerate towards Quorn with a Travelling Post Office train. *Photograph by Warwick Falconer.*

Ex-Great Western Manor Class locomotive 'Ditcheat Manor' number 7821 heads a train of box vans. Whilst passenger trains are slowing here for the station, the Manor is still working hard. *Photograph by Matt Allen.*

Quorn and Woodhouse Station. The central staircase that leads down from the road is clearly visible; this is a classic Great Central feature. *Photograph by Matt Allen.*

The station is magically restored to 1940s' condition including this
recreation of a station master's office. *Photograph by Matt Allen.*

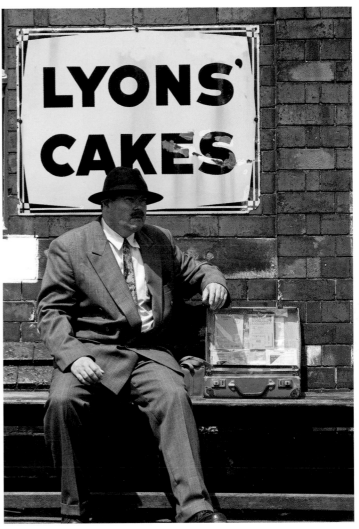

During a 'War on the Line' event some of the re-enactors take a rest. These events are extremely popular with lots of visitors coming to see the period vehicles, re-enactments and even fly-pasts by the 'Battle of Britain Memorial Flight'. *Photograph by Matt Allen.*

You never know whom you'll meet at Quorn and Woodhouse during a 'War on the Line' event! *Photograph by Matt Allen.*

Above:
A 10mph speed limit applies on the nearside track, meanwhile 'Oliver Cromwell' heads south.
Photograph by Matt Allen.

Left:
70048 (70013 renumbered) accelerating away from Quorn and Woodhouse Station. The station is a single island platform with a track either side, a typical Great Central station design. Both Loughborough and Rothley also follow this style. *Photograph by Matt Allen.*

Taken from the same position as the previous photograph but facing in the opposite direction, looking south toward Rothley. 35030 (35005 in disguise) is seen sporting an 'Atlantic Coast Express' headboard, clearly a Waterloo to Devon train has taken a wrong turn! *Photograph by Warwick Falconer.*

A Travelling Post Office drop is about to take place at Quorn. The mailbags can be seen hanging from the apparatus whilst the TPO train accelerates towards it. The TPO apparatus is set up at the far end of the station complex, which gives plenty of room for members of the public to witness the mail exchange. *Photograph by Matt Allen.*

Exchange imminent. You can clearly see that the apparatus on the second coach is ready to catch the mailbag. The TPO run allows trains to travel faster than the 25mph usually permitted for passenger trains at the railway. *Photograph by Matt Allen.*

With lovely low winter light 48305 is coupled to one of the freight trains that are kept in the siding at Quorn. *Photograph by Warwick Falconer.*

Looking south
from Quorn on a
frosty morning.
*Photograph
by Tom Ingall.*

The section of line south of Quorn is very straight. Here 78109 is heading for Rothley, with the Quorn and Woodhouse Station site clearly visible in the background. *Photograph by Matt Allen.*

4141 is facing north for this photograph taken in a field adjacent to the line south of Quorn. Trains can pick up the low winter light beautifully on this section of track. *Photograph by Matt Allen*.

The zoom lens gives the false impression that I'm standing on the track for this photograph of 44422, heading south with a Sunday lunchtime dining train. *Photograph by Matt Allen.*

South of Quorn is another part of the line where silhouettes are possible. You need to pick your spot very carefully as there are a lot of trees and bushes to block the view. 42968 is caught perfectly during a photographers' charter. *Photograph by Warwick Falconer.*

Class 45 diesel locomotives like D123 would have been commonplace in the East Midlands during their time with British Railways. The headcode of 8C30 indicates a slow freight train. *Photograph by Matt Allen.*

42968 has the signal and permission to head south. *Photograph by Warwick Falconer.*

35030 (35005 renumbered) completed with LCGB (Locomotive Club of Great Britain) and 'The Great Central Headboard' recreates a railtour that ran over the line in its final days before the original closure. This was recreated for a photographers' special.
Photograph by Warwick Falconer.

80105 is seen at probably the most popular photographer's haunt on the line, Kinchley Lane. At this spot there is a large bank where photographers can perch as the trains round the curve midway between Quorn and Rothley.
Photograph by Warwick Falconer

I could have filled a book with just pictures taken at Kinchley Lane! I've made the selection carefully to try and get a variety of locomotives and rolling stock. The Class 31 diesel is seen here rounding the curve in charge of a mineral train. *Photograph by Matt Allen.*

Catching the moment. As a photographer you have to be very lucky indeed to get the trains to pass at exactly the same point; here 44422 passes 48305. The GCR is the only heritage railway in the UK where you can be travelling on a steam train and pass another steam-powered train travelling in the opposite direction, as seen here. *Photograph by Matt Allen.*

48305 has had two spells at the Great Central Railway. During its British Railways days it spent time allocated to Wellingborough, Northampton, Crewe South and finally Liverpool Speke Junction engine sheds. In this photograph the 8F is facing north. *Photograph by Warwick Falconer.*

78019 comes into view at the head of a demonstration parcels train that contains a variety of different vehicles.
Photograph by Matt Allen.

The rollerblind says destination 'Rothley' as the Class 101 DMU rounds the corner at Kinchley Lane. The versatile diesel units were seen all over the British Rail system.
Photograph by Matt Allen.

There are various vantage points for the photographer at Kinchley Lane, either up on the bank, closer in from the lineside or even off the road bridge that crosses the line. This photograph of 4953 is taken from the lineside. *Photograph by Matt Allen.*

Reputedly the first locomotive to reach 100mph, number 3440 'City of Truro' was a brief visitor to the railway. The locomotive is another owned by the National Railway Museum and spends its time touring the many heritage railways in the UK. *Photograph by Matt Allen.*

A variation at Kinchley Lane is the 'going away' shot; in winter a lovely glint where the light reflects down the train is possible. Here 4141 hauling a train of maroon coaches picks up the light perfectly. *Photograph by Matt Allen.*

Freight locomotive 4F number 44422 looks perfectly at home with the windcutter mineral wagons. *Photograph by Matt Allen.*

At Kinchley Lane it is quite possible to find anything up to a hundred photographers present when special events are being held, parking being a real problem. However, here ex-GWR Prairie number 4141 scurries past with a mixed rake of coaches on a quiet winter's day. *Photograph by Matt Allen.*

Above:
The next location on our journey is Rabbit Bridge; this is a lovely location as the line curves around from Kinchley Lane heading for Swithland Viaduct. This location is only accessible for photographers that hold lineside passes. 'Leander' is resplendent in its LMS Crimson Lake livery creating a splash of colour. *Photograph by Matt Allen.*

Left:
In this final photograph from Kinchley Lane 'Sir Lamiel' catches some lovely winter light as it rounds the curve. *Photograph by Matt Allen.*

A vantage point slightly further back sees 48305, the single lamp in the middle of the smokebox indicating a headcode for a stopping passenger train. *Photograph by Warwick Falconer.*

Exactly the same train as in the previous photograph but 'going away', the parapet of the Swithland Viaduct is just in view. *Photograph by Warwick Falconer.*

Above:
Again the same train is caught 'going away', the guard can be seen at the rear of the brake van.
Also visible is the edge of Swithland Reservoir, an area of real interest along the line. *Photograph by Matt Allen.*

Left:
This particular day was extremely frustrating, a photographers' special with very little sun.
However, whilst at Rabbit Bridge the sun did appear illuminating 70048 (70013 renumbered)
and its mixed freight train perfectly. *Photograph by Matt Allen.*

42968 passes under the bridge with a train destined for Leicester North. *Photograph by Warwick Falconer.*

'King Arthur' number 30777 heads a train that features a Travelling Post Office coach at the front, an LNER teak vehicle and a Mk1 coach, creating a very varied train formation. *Photograph by Warwick Falconer.*

This shot is taken from an area that is normally out of bounds, special permission being sought for this photographers' special. 30777 with a matching train of green coaches is approaching Swithland Viaduct.
Photograph by Warwick Falconer.

Swithland Viaduct is actually a series of viaducts spanning Swithland Reservoir. Getting a clear view of the viaduct is not easy as a lot of the surrounding land is out of bounds, however some artistic photographs are achievable. *Photograph by Matt Allen.*

The viaduct itself is prohibited to photographers due to very tight clearances, however a photographers' special gives the opportunity for some rare photographs. *Photograph by Matt Allen.*

The engine is actually 63601, with the last train from Loughborough to Leicester on a winter's day.
Photograph by Matt Allen.

Sunset at Swithland. Some wonderful sunsets can be achieved across the reservoir. This photograph was taken during a Winter Steam Gala, with the sun dropping fast, the train (4141) only just turning up in time.
Photograph by Matt Allen.

The train has now crossed Swithland Reservoir and is beginning its approach to Swithland sidings. Jubilee number 5690 'Leander' visited the line for a short time. With a scene like this I wish it had stayed for longer!
Photograph by Matt Allen.

126

4141 is pulling into Swithland sidings, where the railway has lots of storage area for rolling stock that is pending or undergoing restoration. Level with the back of the train you can see the signal gantries but devoid of signal arms.
Photograph by Matt Allen.

'Oliver Cromwell' pulls into Swithland sidings; visible to the right is a clearance, which is the proposed branchline to Mountsorrel.
Photograph by Matt Allen.

In the same location as the previous photograph but with leaves still on the trees, 'Leander' continues its journey to Leicester.
Photograph by Matt Allen.

The signal box at Swithland is due to be commissioned shortly, which will allow for a much more effective control of traffic. At Swithland the mainline tracks pass through the middle with sidings used for storage on either side. Stanier Mogul 42968 passes the signal box on a clear winter's day.
Photograph by Warwick Falconer.

128

Further down the siding 45305 passes through, although it is now resident at the Great Central. This locomotive was a part of a class that totalled 842 locomotives and was one of the lucky survivors. *Photograph by Matt Allen*.

The approach to Rothley Station is in a cutting, here 70048 (70013 renumbered) comes through the cutting with plenty of steam evident. *Photograph by Matt Allen.*

Above:
35030 'Elder Dempster Lines' (actually 35005 'Canadian Pacific') heads north from Rothley.
Photograph by Warwick Falconer.

Left:
Taken from the road bridge at Rothley Station, 78019 is waiting at the signal to depart north whilst 63601 on the windcutters heads south. 78019 is actually on a 'Driver Experience' where members of the public can pay to drive and fire a steam locomotive.
Photograph by Matt Allen.

With threatening skies Q6 locomotive number 63395 makes
the approach to Rothley. *Photograph by Matt Allen.*

Disguised 35005 'Canadian Pacific' running as 35030 'Elder Dempster Lines' hauls a train that features two parcel vehicles at the front away from Rothley, the locomotive facing north towards Leicester. *Photograph by Matt Allen*.

Rothley Station. Complete with signal box on the left and 'Ellis's Tearoom' on the right, the station complex is a compact affair. The usual road bridge with a staircase dropping down to a single platform is evident. 63601 has just pulled into the station with a train for Leicester North.
Photograph by Matt Allen.

Rothley Station is restored to Edwardian condition complete with original gas lamps.
Photograph by Matt Allen.

One of the waiting
rooms at Rothley Station.
Photograph by Matt Allen.

Summer flowers complete the scene at Rothley Station; Ellis's Tearoom
(a great stop for a railway photographer!) can be seen in the background.
Photograph by Matt Allen.

'The train at platform two is for Quorn and Woodhouse and Loughborough Central only'.
Photograph by Matt Allen.

The central staircase that gives access to Rothley platform from the road. This arrangement with single platform is the same at Loughborough and Quorn and Woodhouse Stations.
Photograph by Matt Allen.

The view from north of the station looking south towards Leicester North. Just visible at the end of the station is the carriage and wagon restoration shed. *Photograph by Matt Allen.*

Rothley Station is packed full of period features, a perfect place to spend an hour or two exploring everything it has to offer. *Photograph by Matt Allen.*

The double track finishes at Rothley, the line on to Leicester North being single track. Merchant Navy 35050 (actually 35005) is heading north on the single track towards Rothley from Leicester North. *Photograph by Warwick Falconer.*

Passing the oak tree at Thurcaston 42968 heads for Leicester North. Railway photographers often neglect the single-track section but it does have a few nice locations like this to offer. *Photograph by Warwick Falconer.*

Above:
Approaching Leicester North Station 5690 'Leander' heads a train with an unusual LNER 'Pigeon Van' at the front. The locomotive was built in March 1936 at Crewe Works. *Photograph by Matt Allen.*

Right:
The water level on the tender of 70048 (actually 70013) is evident as it sits in the platform at Leicester North, the end of the eight mile journey from Loughborough. *Photograph by Matt Allen.*

Leicester North Station is actually the site of 'Belgrave and Birstall Station' as it was called during the original Great Central days. In this photograph of 63601 you can see the road bridge and the original entrance to the platform. The platform has been re-constructed slightly further south and isn't of the original single island platform design. *Photograph by Matt Allen.*

35030 (actually 35005) waits to leave Leicester North with the journey north to Loughborough ahead of it. *Photograph by Warwick Falconer.*

142

Leaving school?

THERE'S A CAREER FOR YOU ON BRITISH RAILWAYS

For boys of 15 years and over, there is a wide variety of jobs available on British Railways in the following Departments:

Commercial	Junior Clerks
Operating	Junior Porters and Signal Lads
Mechanical & Electrical	Apprentices in many specific trades
Carriage & Wagon	Apprentices in many specific trades
Signal Engineering	Trade Apprentices and Probationers
Civil Engineering	Apprentices in several trades
Motive Power	Engine Cleaners and Apprentices

For Grammar and Public schoolboys who have the right qualifications there are special training courses in the Civil, Mechanical & Electrical and Signal Engineering departments

For further information, consult your local Youth Employment Officer or your Careers Master at school, or write, stating your particular interest, to:

REGIONAL ESTABLISHMENT & STAFF OFFICER BRITISH RAILWAYS

Eastern Region, Liverpool Street Station, London E.C.2
London Midland Region, Euston Station, London N.W.1
North Eastern Region, Headquarters Offices, York
Scottish Region, 302 Buchanan Street, Glasgow, C.3
Southern Region, Waterloo Station, London S.E.1
Western Region, Paddington Station, London W.2

Leaving school? I'm not sure the railways can offer the opportunities shown on this poster these days, however the new Great Central Railway has lots of opportunities to offer volunteers with spare time on their hands.
Photograph by Matt Allen.

End of the line. Leicester North is the end of line – in this photograph you can see a new station canopy being built. This is one of many new developments as the Great Central Railway continues to move forward 'Double Track Style'.
Photograph by Matt Allen.